99c
COMPLETE

INITIALED CEDAR CHEST
with 6 Dainty Embroidered Hankies

The graduate way to present 'kerchiefs—in handsome aromatic cedar chest she can use for other 'knick-knacks.' The six 10½-inch hankies are lace-trimmed lovelies with dainty hand-looped embroidery on fine Combed Cotton Lawn, ridged hemstitched hems. Initialed 7 x 5 chest has lock and key. PRINT initials for 'Kerchiefs of White with assorted embroidery.
8 A U28—Shpg. wt. 1 lb. 8 ozs.

EXQUISITE LACE CORNERS!
In Lovely Gift Box

3 FOR 59c

Among our loveliest 'kerchiefs—worthy of the most particular lady on your list. Made of cleverest, softest, finest Combed Cotton Lawn, with rich lace, gay hand-looped embroidery and dainty ridged hemstitched hems. To be presentably beautiful hinged gift box. Color—White with 3 tone embroidery.
8 A U22—Size about 10½ inches.
Shpg. wt. 12 ozs.

FINE FRENCH LACE T
In Unusual Novelty Fol

3 FOR 49c

The minute she opens the folder you made the right selection—[?] on the smiling face. The dainties and hand-embroidered corners, 'kerchiefs of fine Combed Cotton La handy folder is lovely enough to k Color—White with 3 color embroidery.
8 A U21—Size about 10½ inche
Shpg. wt. 10 ozs.

DELIGHTFUL GIFT SET
THRIFTY PRICED!

25c

A bright Combo dy for her pocket a cute nosey or ment for her cut of idea!—a bottle of sweet smelling Jasmine perfume to add her. Holiday mood! All packed in cellophane-windowed box and filled with gift card. And all for a few pennies. Put several on gift list.
8 A U27—Hanky in assorted color prints.
Shpg. wt. 12 ozs.

GAILY EMBROIDERED
PURE LINEN

3 FOR 29c

Pure Irish linen 'kerchiefs are in a class by themselves—and these delightfully embroidered ones are a first-class bargain. Good Quality. Hemstitched hems. Color—White with 3 tone embroidery.
8 A U26—Size about 10½ ins.
Shpg. wt. 8 ozs.

COLORFULLY EMBROIDERED
LACY CORNERS

3 FOR 25c

Not often can you buy 'kerchiefs with hand-looped embroidery and lacy corners for so little! Of Combed Cotton Lawn with ridged hemstitched hems.
Color—White with 3 tone embroidery.
8 A U24—Size about 10½ ins.
Shpg. wt. 8 ozs.

PERSONALIZE
EMBROIDERED

3 FOR 2

Big embroidered for that 'personal Combed Cotton L hemstitched hems. No I O O U Y Color—White with 3 initials. Size about
8 A U23—Shpg. w

Uh-oh,
Mom
has that look.

Uh-oh,
Mom
has that look.

A lighthearted look at our Family Tree
by David Butler

**Andrews McMeel
Publishing**

Kansas City

Who says superheroes are make-believe?
I know a woman who can read minds, see
through walls, predict the future, carry a
household, fold time, become invisible, and
alter reality. It's my mom.

Oh, and you should see what she does
AFTER breakfast.

I get tired just watching her. Her mind is a
tightly wound clock that spins off priorities like
a pinwheel in a hurricane.

She can take care of all the world's problems, while
making sure we're not a part of them.

Although she admits to having her Kryptonite.
She calls it
"The mind of man."

Dad never found that to be funny.

Mom is the ideal empowered woman. She's sure of herself and works diligently to protect and preserve her family and her way of life. She maintains dignity and spirit, and inspires all of us who walk in her shadow.

She just can't figure out the VCR.

But like the mother lion, she keeps her cubs in check.
And by so doing, keeps the world in check.
After all, you can't round a corner without running
into someone else's mom.
And the moms are all connected through
the mom grapevine.

Her powerful maternal instincts are not hindered by boundary. What I mean by this is that we can't get away with anything, no matter where we are.

I

And even if we could, the unshakable
"Guilt of the Overlooking Mother Spirit"
would be there to grab us by the scruff of the neck.
Mom's power transcends time and space.

And yet on occasion we stretch the boundaries
of her benevolence. We "exceed the legal speed limit"
of Mom's infinite compassion.

And then it happens.

"Uh-oh. Mom has that look."

Whereas Dad's inclination is toward a direct approach ("you are grounded"), Mom tends to favor the uncertain future direction or, as we've come to know it, the "Vague Life Upheaval."

Herein life is established as a matter of what-ifs, as in, "What if you continue down this path of chaos?"; "You'll pay the price!"; "You and I are going to go round and round!"

Of course, we never want to find out what any of this means. And so we straighten up.

As we've come to understand it, reality is what Mom makes it. And in Mom's reality, there is no time for shenanigans, hooligans, roughhousing, lip, sass, smart talk, attitude, or laziness.

APR 1966

Without her keen sense of direction
where would we be?

Still sitting in front of the TV, watching cartoons in
our pajamas, holding a lukewarm bowl of Cap'n Crunch
at three in the afternoon, I would imagine.

Fortunately, Mom knows how to get us going.
And she knows how to have fun. Just when you think
her life has always been about being a mom, you find
out that she's had some background prior to your
existence. Like field hockey, or golf, or baseball, or
target shooting.

And she can beat you blindfolded!

Forget about playing cards—she'll kill you.

When you have a basic understanding of
multitasking that puts the average CEO to shame,
counting cards isn't that complicated.

But you know and I know that Mom has let us win more times than we can count. Just so we could get a taste of it and understand how to do it with humility and compassion.

Dad, on the other hand. . .

AUG · 73

That's one of many of Mom's superpowers. A sense of knowing what is right for us, even when we don't understand, and the ability to help us see even when we don't realize we're being guided.

She says she's "just keeping it together," but we know that she can handle life's balance beam just fine. Her modesty is a thin disguise for her indomitable spirit.

Mom adds creativity and charm to the everyday things. Her keen eye and seemingly never-ending compendium of design ideas keep the house awhirl in "kinetic artistic expression."

Which means we have to paint again. And again.

But that's all a part of Mom changing the world.

ONE BEDROOM AT A TIME!

And if it wasn't for her, imagine what
the bathroom would look like.

Yep, you don't realize exactly how much Mom does on a day-to-day basis until you move away from home. How quickly our lives go to pot once we move out.

I didn't realize in high school that I had a guardian, a full-time chef, a laundry service, a benevolent loan officer, emergency roadside service, free room and board, a cornucopia of food and dry goods, and a clean, healthy environment to enjoy it all in.

I've been in some really nice hotels, none of which offer half of the above.

Plus, you get a fantastic, witty, and charming best
friend as your full-time companion.
It's amazing to me that anyone would ever
want to screw that up!

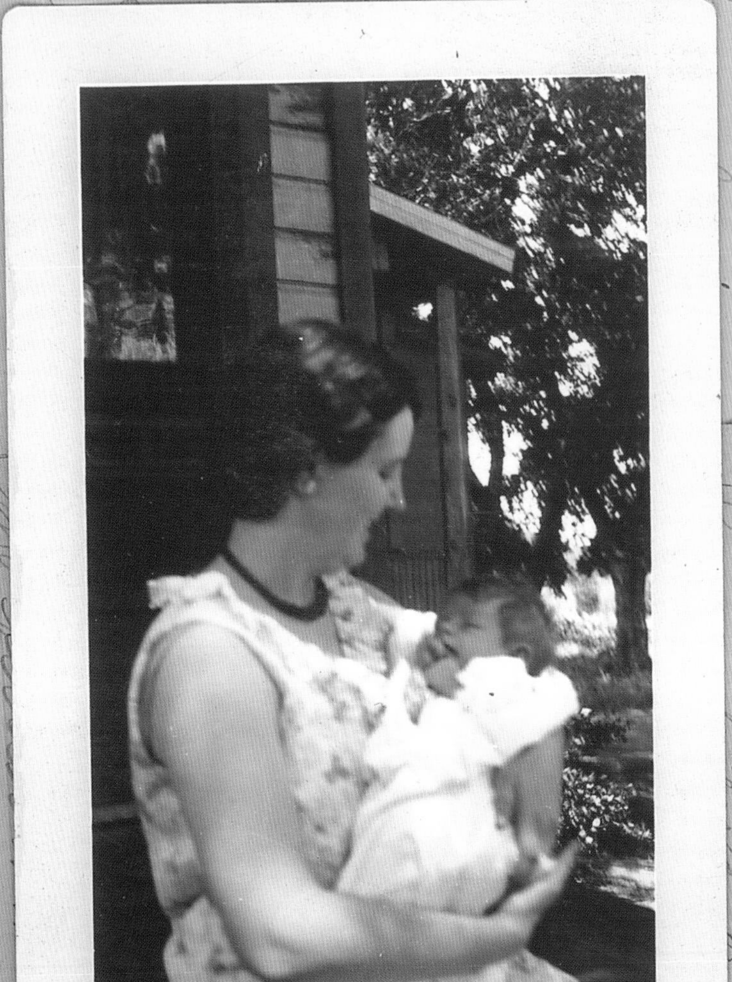

But that's the beauty. You might not see until you go away. The fact that a woman who held the key to your life for so long and who had the responsibility to merely keep you alive until you could fend for yourself will always have that part of your soul. The vulnerable and loving part that she helped to create.

Now, that part of you that likes to run down the
street waving a pointed stick at the neighbors yelling,
"The pirates have taken the ship!". . .
She doesn't have any idea where that came from.
At least it's not from her side of the family.

Granted, Mom seems pretty sweet now, but go ahead and ask her about her checkered youth. It'll probably make your adolescent antics sound like an episode of the Mickey Mouse Club.

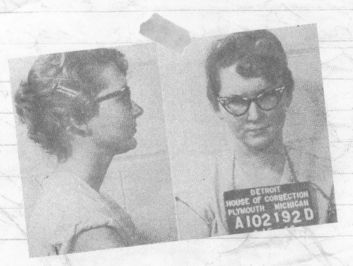

Which is to say, although there have been some amazing breakthroughs in technology over the last few decades, Mom has been through all the phases of life that we're going through and it's not that different. The face of emotional, physical, and mental challenges won't change over the decades. Heartbreak and happiness are the same today as they were thirty years ago.

That's why we take Mom's advice.

She can see the potential in each of us and
understands the steps to reaching our goals.

Each step in the right direction will
bring us that much closer.

There are no shortcuts.

Continue in a consistent path with
right-mindedness.

Oh, and wipe your feet.

It's amazing that one person so full of imagination, passion, and caring spirit could be so worried about a little dirt.

And it's just that type of smart-aleck
attitude that will keep me from doing
anything with my life.

Now, how does she expect me to
"Wipe that smirk off of my face"?

Mom seems to have all manner of friendships too.
All of Dad's friends seem like Dad.
But Mom's friends run the gamut of different
personalities and traits. They're a very colorful bunch.
Apparently, that's why Mom spends so much time
talking about them, to each other, at different
times, on touchy topics, on the phone, right when
I need something.

Mom. Mom. Mom. Mom. Mom. Mom. Mom. Mom. Mom. Mom. Mom. Mom. Mom.

Uh-oh. Mom has that look.

Amazingly, Mom has a life "outside" of us.
This just adds to the quandary of her existence.
Superheroes have friends? Apparently so. Other
supermoms. Trading supermom tips and helpful hints,
letting each other in on the big secret.
Or maybe just looking for an escape pod.

That's part of Mom's vibrant life. Keeping things
interesting while maintaining her practical side. She is
a woman, after all! You can't be a mom with blinders
on. To know the world is to know oneself. That's why
she loves cable TV.

Just think, without Mom we wouldn't understand
these simple concepts: throw rugs, coasters,
disinfectant, milk, tetanus, coordinating outfits,
socks, combs, tissues, vegetables, moderation, guest
towels, bleach, conservation, potpourri, hampers,
compassion, toenail clippers, comforters, crafts,
and humility.

Dad still doesn't get most of those.

And in the face of particular mom
stereotypes we see various anomalies
and outstanding personal skills.

My amazing mother can:

go to a party in a dress that she already owns wearing
shoes she purchased over a year ago

safely drive and park a car

handle a remote control

watch a ball game

produce any category of prying object
from her bottomless purse

survive without a cell phone, pager, or computer

compliment EVERYONE on their
appearance regardless of their state

curse like a sailor

find staggering bargains

and call upon an internal keen sense of direction.

With such self-motivated adaptability my mom proves
once again that even in a pink cowl-neck mohair
sweater, you can be one tough cookie.

And if you wear it with white pants after
Labor Day, you'd better be.

From her humor we find joy.
From her spirit we draw confidence.
From her imagination we learn creativity.
And from her patience we learn balance.

Oh, and from her cooking we learn curiosity.

Mostly we stand in awe of Mom, as the amazing
superhero who constantly exceeds our demands and
awakens in us the truth of love. She's our spiritual
leader and benevolent guide, pointing us ever forward
while making sure we look at ourselves along the way.
She's the friend to end all friends, who brought us
into this amazing world. . .

apparently just so we could do
her housework!

First published by MQ Publications Limited
12 The Ivories, 6–8 Northampton Street,
London N1 2HY

Copyright © 2002 by MQ Publications Limited

Text copyright © 2002 by David Butler
Design by Art of the Midwest Studio

ISBN 0-7407-2273-5

Library of Congress Control Number: 2001095905

Printed and bound in China

Credit for You . . . SEE PAGE 7

48c

as, look at ~~an 60c for a~~ ~~lece~~ dresser-~~thrill~~ any girl ~~to~~ her toes. ~~r~~, brush, and ~~position~~; gift ~~due.~~ ~~ik~~ ~~sou~~ Glue ~~te~~ color. ~~1 lb.~~

Gilt-Decorated $100
Initialed

A full-sized set, priced specially low. The gilt initial and scrolls are very effective on the Mother-of-Pearl Composition backs. Mirror 14 inches long; brush and comb in proportion. Rayon-lined gift box. Order early.
Colors— Blue
Jade-green Rose } State color.
8 H G 1 3—Please PRINT initial.
Shpg. wt. 2 lbs. 2 ozs.

Gold-Plated Trim $298
Richly Embossed

Crystal-effect handles. Gleaming, expertly fashioned, glass handles reflect every ray of light, to make this dresser-set a perfect jewel. Gold-plated edges and filigree-patterned shield. Composition backs. 12-inch mirror with beveled glass; comb, brush. Rayon-lined gift case. Colors—Ivory, Blue, Green, Rose, all with crystal-clear handles.
8 E G 1 6—A "1940" style-set.
Shpg. wt. 5 lbs. 10 ozs.

Deluxe 7-Piece Set $3
Gold-Plated Trim

Excited eyes, a whispered "Wonderful" will thank you for this set. The handles and trim, Yellow Gold-plated, are elaborately embossed to look hand-etched. 13-inch mirror has a clear, beveled glass. Delicately shaded Composition backs; gorgeous 11-inch hair tray. Powder jar, cream jar, and nail, too. Really its BEAUTIFUL.
Colors—Ivory, Blue, or Green. State color.
8 E G 1 8—Our Finest for Your Dear One.
Shpg. wt. 6 lbs. 8 ozs.

Every Woman Wants one of these Sets!

FOR OTHER BARGAINS SEE
Fall and Winter Catalog 1939-1940